A Robbie Reader

Meet Our New Student From

AUSTRALIA

Ann Weil

Mitchell Lane
PUBLISHERS

P.O. Box 196
Hockessin, Delaware 19707
Visit us on the web: www.mitchelllane.com
Comments? email us: mitchelllane@mitchelllane.com

Meet Our New Student From

Australia • China • Colombia • Great Britain • Haiti •
Israel • Korea • Malaysia • Mexico •
New Zealand • Nigeria • Tanzania

For my own little Aussie, Alice.
 –Love, Mom

PUBLISHER'S NOTE: The facts on which the story
in this book is based have been thoroughly
researched. Documentation of such research
can be found on page 44. While every possible
effort has been made to ensure accuracy, the
publisher will not assume liability for damages
caused by inaccuracies in the data, and
makes no warranty on the accuracy of the
information contained herein.

**Library of Congress Cataloging-in-Publication
Data**
Weil, Ann.
  Meet our new student from Australia / by
Ann Weil.
     p. cm.—(A Robbie reader)
  Includes bibliographical references and
index.
  ISBN 978-1-58415-652-9 (library bound)
  1. Australia—Juvenile literature. I. Title.
DU96.W43 2008
994—dc22
                                          2008002267

Printing 1   2   3   4   5   6   7   8   9

PLB

CONTENTS

Koalas live in the wild in Australia. They are sometimes called koala bears, but koalas are not a kind of bear. They are marsupials (mar-SOO-pee-uls), like kangaroos. Marsupials are mammals that have a pouch in which to carry their babies.

A Girl from Oz

Chapter

Hi. My name is Stacey O'Neal. I've lived in Walpole, New Hampshire, my whole life. I'm eight and a half years old and just started third grade. Today, our teacher, Mrs. Young, had some great news. She told us that we were getting a new classmate.

"I hope it's a girl," I said to myself. There are only three other girls in my class, and they've been best friends since they were born. Sometimes I feel left out.

"Her name is Abby Hamilton," continued Mrs. Young.

"Yes!" I said, out loud this time. Everyone turned to look at me.

". . . and she's an Aussie," Mrs. Young finished. It sounded like "Ozzie."

"Is she from Oz?" asked Hamza.

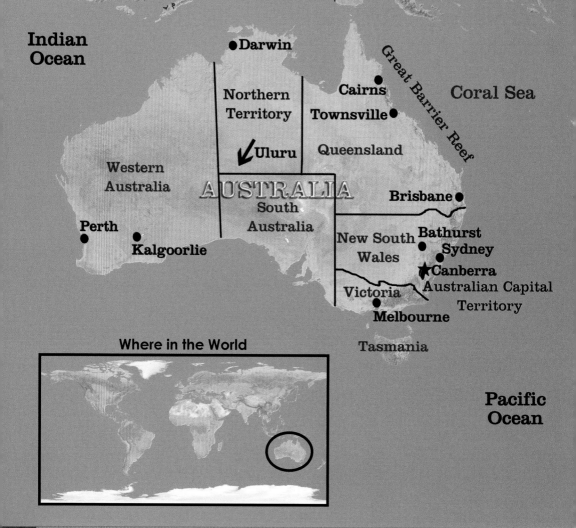

INDONESIA

PAPUA NEW GUINEA

Indian Ocean

●Darwin

Northern Territory

Cairns

Townsville●

Coral Sea

Great Barrier Reef

↙Uluru

Queensland

Western Australia

AUSTRALIA

South Australia

Brisbane●

Perth
●

Kalgoorlie
●

New South Wales

Bathurst
●

Sydney
●

★Canberra

Australian Capital Territory

Victoria

Melbourne
●

Pacific Ocean

Tasmania

Where in the World

FACTS ABOUT AUSTRALIA

Total area: 2,967,909 square miles (slightly smaller than 48 connected U.S. states)
Population: 20,434,176 (July 2007 est.)
Capital City: Canberra
Religions: Catholicism, Anglicanism, other forms of Christianity; Buddhism; Islam

Official Language: English
Chief Exports: Coal, gold, meat, wool, alumina, iron ore, wheat, machinery, and transportation equipment
Monetary Unit: Australian Dollar

"An Aussie is someone from Australia," Mrs. Young explained.

"Where's Australia?" asked Emma.

"Does she speak English?" asked Luke.

"What's school like in Australia?" asked Patrick.

"Can she sit next to me?" I said.

Mrs. Young walked to the big world map we have on the wall and pointed out Australia.

"It's an island," said Carrie.

"Yes," said Mrs. Young. "Australia is a country and a **continent**. We'll study Australia this week. That way we'll know some things about Australia

> ### *fun* FACTS
>
> Koalas have TWO thumbs on each front paw. They also have very sharp claws. Although they can quickly climb trees, koalas can't run very fast on the ground.

before Abby arrives. So, let's get started. What do you already know about Australia?" she asked the class.

"There are kangaroos," said Emma, "and koalas."

"There are crocodiles and snakes," said Josh.

"And sharks!" added Luke.

Mrs. Young wrote the names of those animals on the board. "Okay, that's enough animals for now. What else do you know about Australia?" she asked.

Chapter 1

The Great Barrier Reef is 1,250 miles long. It comes to within three miles of the coast of Australia. It is alive with fish and coral, but large patches of coral have been dying. Scientists believe the coral is suffering from higher water temperatures caused by global warming.

"The Great Barrier Reef is in Australia," I said. I watched a show about the Great Barrier Reef on television. I loved seeing all the colorful fish that lived in the reef.

Mrs. Young wrote *Great Barrier Reef* next to the list of animals. "What else?" she asked.

No one raised a hand. I guess we had a lot to learn about Australia.

"We'll learn about the history of Australia, the land, the people, and the climate," Mrs. Young said.

"What does *climate* mean?" asked Luke.

"Climate is the usual weather in a place," explained Mrs. Young. Then she told us that we would work in pairs and prepare a report about one topic to present to the class. I'd be working with Emma. Our topic was the history of Australia. I already had an idea.

"Let's make a timeline," I suggested to Emma.

"Yes!" Emma agreed. "Our timeline can show when important events happened."

"Let's make a really big timeline," I added. "That way we will have room for lots of pictures." We started making a list of what we would need for our project.

Next we had library period. Everyone looked for books about Australia. I went on the Internet and printed out some great pictures. I couldn't wait to get started!

Australia

The didgeridoo (or didge, for short) is a long flute. Aboriginal people use it to make music like sounds they hear in nature. It makes a low sound, called a drone.

From Dreamtime to
Democracy

Chapter **2**

The first Australians are called **Aborigines** (aa-buh-RIH-jih-nees). They have lived in Australia for at least 40,000 years, and some people think they have been there for much longer. They did not farm, or build towns or cities. They lived close to nature, moving from place to place to gather food that grew naturally. They hunted, too.

There were many different groups of Aborigines that lived all over Australia. They spoke different languages, but they did not write things down. One custom they all had in common was sharing stories. Their stories told of a time long ago when **ancestor** (AN-ses-tor) spirits, often in the form of animals, created the land and people of Australia. That time and those stories are called the Dreamtime.

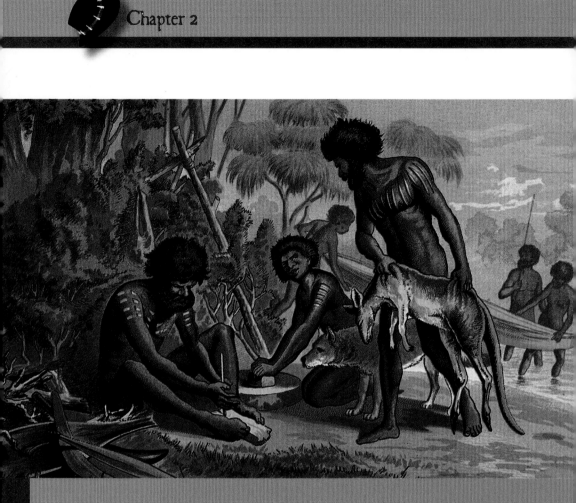

Australia's Aboriginal people were hunters and gatherers. They were also skilled with many types of tools. They used stone tools for sharpening knives, to grind seed, and to prepare animal skins. Tribes along the coast would tip their spears with sharp fishbones.

Aboriginal people believed the Dreamtime stories really happened. They saw the proof of the stories in the land. They celebrated Dreamtime in music, art, and dance.

First Settlers

In the 1600s, European explorers discovered Australia. An explorer named James Cook claimed the land for England in the 1700s.

The first white settlers came from England. They were **convicts** and their jailors. Many of the convicts were poor people who had stolen food to feed their families. English jails were too full, so the convicts were put on ships, bound for the new **colony**.

It took months at sea to reach Australia. The first convict ships left England in 1787. They arrived in January 1788.

The English pushed Aborigines off the land where they were living. Many Aborigines got sick from European diseases and died. Others were killed. The survivors set up new homes in the hot, dry middle of the country.

Gold Rush

The Australian gold rush began in the 1850s. A man discovered a tiny bit of gold in Bathurst, New South Wales. He knew about the gold rush in America. He guessed that Australia had a lot of gold, too—and he was right.

Cassilis was once the largest gold mining town in Victoria. Besides the mining operation, it also had a school, hotels, a bakery, banks, and post offices. By 1917, after the gold was gone, Cassilis became a ghost town.

Thousands of people came to Australia from all over the world to look for gold. People came from North America, Europe, and China. The number of people doubled. Then it doubled again. More gold was discovered farther south, in the state of Victoria. Suddenly there was plenty of money. New cities sprang up. Soon, Australia had its first railway.

In the 1890s, a huge amount of gold was found in Western Australia. People rushed there to make their fortune. But that part of Australia is desert, and there was not enough water for people to drink.

Perth, hundreds of miles away on the west coast, had plenty of water. A pipeline was built, and water flowed through it for more than 300 miles from Perth to Kalgoorlie (kal-GOO-lee). This was an amazing achievement.

Long Live the Queen!

America fought for independence from England. Australia never did. In 1901, Australia joined the British Commonwealth of Nations. It is still part of the Commonwealth. (Canada is, too.) This means that the Queen of England is the official Head of State of Australia. However, the Queen of England does not make the laws.

Australia has its own government, called a democracy. People there vote for their own leaders. The Australian government is not the same as the **democracy** in the United States of America. It is more like the government in England. Australia does not have a president. It has a prime minister instead. The Parliament of Australia includes the Senate and House of Representatives.

Australia

Sydney is the oldest and largest city in Australia. It is home to more than 4 million people.

The Land
Down Under

Chapter **3**

Hundreds of millions of years ago, Australia was part of a huge landmass called Gondwana (gond-WAH-nah). This landmass included Antarctica, Africa, India, and other places. Slowly, big pieces of land broke away. At first, Australia was still connected to Antarctica. Then, about 50 million years ago, it split off on its own.

Australia is the only country that is its own continent. It is almost as big as the United States, but Australia looks and feels very different from America. Most of Australia is hot, dry, and flat. Because it is so far south of the equator, it is known as the Land Down Under.

In 2008, about 21 million people were living in Australia. (The population of the United States is more than 300 million.) Nine out of ten Australians live in cities near the ocean. Only a small fraction (about 7 percent) of Australia is farmland.

Into the Outback

Millions of years ago, the center of Australia was a great sea. Now it is desert, called the Outback. Red dirt roads stretch for hundreds of miles without a house in sight.

The Australian Outback is too dry for many people to live there, yet it is full of wildlife. Red kangaroos and lizards abound, as do poisonous (POY-sun-us) snakes and spiders.

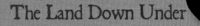

Uluru, or Ayers Rock, is one of the best-known natural features in Australia. As the sun rises and sets, the rock seems to change color, from red to orange to pale purple.

Australia gets very little rain. There are no big lakes or rivers in the center. It is the driest continent that has people living on it.

Uluru, a huge red rock, stands in the desert. It rises 1,100 feet above sea level. Uluru is its traditional name.

It is also called Ayers Rock, after Sir Henry Ayers. It is a **sacred** place for Aboriginal people.

People come from all over the world to see Uluru. Many climb up to the top, but Aboriginal people do not. They believe it is wrong for people to walk on sacred ground. There are signs asking people not to climb Uluru. Many visitors go up to the top anyway.

Great Barrier Reef

The Great Barrier Reef is the largest natural feature on Earth. Astronauts can see it when they are orbiting the planet. People love to dive and snorkel at the reef. It is a beautiful, interesting place.

*fun*FACTS

The Great Barrier Reef includes more than 2,600 different kinds of coral. Coral grows only a few inches each year.

Many animals make the reef their home. There are about 1,500 different kinds of fish. Sea mammals, such as whales, dolphins, and porpoises, live there, too. There are giant clams, sea turtles, sea snakes, and more than 200 kinds of birds.

Coral reefs may look like colorful rocks, but they are actually colonies of tiny animals. The reefs are home to many kinds of fish. About one-third of all fish species live in coral reefs.

There are more than 60 different kinds of kangaroos. Large kangaroos live in the wild only in Australia. They are the country's symbol. Baby kangaroos are called joeys. Males are called bucks, boomers, or jacks, and females are called does, flyers, or jills.

Drought

Drought—a long period without rain—is part of Australia's unique climate. Because of droughts, people all over Australia cannot take water for granted. There are rules about how they can use it. In

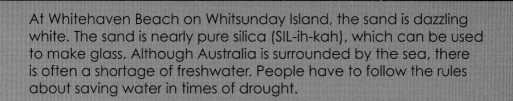

At Whitehaven Beach on Whitsunday Island, the sand is dazzling white. The sand is nearly pure silica (SIL-ih-kah), which can be used to make glass. Although Australia is surrounded by the sea, there is often a shortage of freshwater. People have to follow the rules about saving water in times of drought.

some places, it is illegal to water lawns. People cannot use a hose to wash their car. They must use a bucket instead.

Sugar is big business in Queensland, Australia. Sugarcane is harvested, then quickly moved to a nearby sugar mill by truck or train, where it is processed into sugar and other products.

Celebrations and Celebrities

Chapter **4**

People in Australia live much like people do in the United States and other **developed** countries. Children begin public school at age four or five. Most schoolchildren wear a school uniform, which includes a broad-brimmed hat to protect them from the strong sun while they are outside at recess. **Unemployment** is low in Australia. Most people have good-paying jobs. They enjoy holidays and vacations. Sports are important, too. Many Australians watch cricket on the "telly." At first, cricket may seem like baseball because there is a pitcher (called a bowler) and someone at bat. But the games are not really similar. A cricket game can go on for days! Fans cheer for the home team against teams from other Australian states. Australian cricket teams also play teams from other countries, including England, New Zealand, Sri

Queensland is crawling with crocodiles. Saltwater crocs, called Salties, tend to be much bigger than freshwater crocs, called Freshies. Taking a dip in a swimming hole is risky unless you are sure there are no crocodiles around. It is safer to see crocs at a zoo.

Lanka, and South Africa. Australians have their own version of football, which they call footy. It is known as Aussie Rules. Soccer and rugby are also popular.

Although there are many things that are the same, life in Australia is still a bit different than life in other parts of the world.

Back to School

Children in Australia get a summer vacation . . . in December and January! Australia is south of the equator, so the seasons are reversed. When it is winter in the United States, it is summer in Australia. The school year begins at the end of January, after their six-week summer vacation.

Christmas in July

December is often the hottest month of the year Down Under. Many Australians celebrate Christmas (December 25) by going to the beach. Still, some want a traditional Christmas dinner, but not in the heat of summer. They celebrate Christmas in July, which is usually the coldest winter month in Australia.

Australian dollars and cents

G'Day, Mate!

Most Australians speak English, but it sounds very different from the English spoken in America. Even the word *Australian* sounds different. Americans say it slowly. They say each part, so the word has three syllables. Australians say it quickly, using only one syllable: *Strine.*

Australians use the British spelling of some words, so *harbor* is spelled *harbour* and *center* is spelled *centre.* Some Australian words are common in England but not in America. They call the trunk of a car the boot. Diapers are called nappies. A trashcan is a bin.

Happy Birthday to You!

People celebrate birthdays in Australia with games and cake and the same "Happy Birthday" song that is sung in the United States. After singing the birthday song, they cheer, "Hip hip hooray!"

A child's birthday party in Australia is not complete without the game called pass the parcel. Before the party, an adult prepares the parcel. A gift is wrapped in many layers of wrapping paper or newspaper. Small toys and candy are hidden in each layer of paper.

When it is time to play, children sit close together in a circle. An adult is in charge of starting and stopping

Colorful fairy bread is served at children's parties all across Australia. Often the bread is cut into triangles, but some people cut different shapes, such as stars or circles. Fairy bread has to have enough sprinkles on each piece so that the pieces don't stick when they're stacked.

the music. When the music starts, the children pass the parcel. When the music stops, whoever is holding the parcel unwraps one layer of paper and gets to keep the small toy or candy. This happens again and again until someone unwraps the last layer of paper and gets to keep the gift inside.

A favorite birthday party snack is fairy bread. It is easy to make. Spread soft butter on a slice of bread.

Sydney Harbour has two famous landmarks. The Sydney Opera House has become a symbol for Australia. It opened in 1973. The Sydney Harbour Bridge is the widest (though not the longest) steel arch bridge in the world. Building began in 1924 and took eight years.

Top with sprinkles. In Australia, sprinkles are called "hundreds and thousands."

Australia Day

Australia Day is celebrated every January 26. It marks the day in 1788 when the first convicts from England landed in Sydney Harbour and built the first colony in Australia.

Australia Day used to be called Anniversary Day. There are Australia Day parades in many towns and cities. It is also a day of protest for some Aboriginal people.

ANZAC Day

April 25 is ANZAC (AN-zak) Day in Australia. ANZAC stands for Australian and New Zealand Army Corps. It is a national holiday, like Memorial Day in the United States, when the country's soldiers are honored.

ANZAC Day began as a way to remember soldiers who fought and died in World War I. Now it is a day to remember all Australian and New Zealand soldiers.

Off to the Races

Horse racing is popular in Australia. One of the biggest races is the Melbourne Cup, held on the first Tuesday in November. That day is a public holiday in the city of Melbourne. People dress up to go to the race. Women wear huge hats. All over Australia, people stop what they are doing to follow the action. It is a fun day for all Australians.

Phar Lap, the Wonder Horse

Phar Lap was a very famous horse. He was born in New Zealand in 1926. His name means "lightning" in the Thai language.

Actor Heath Ledger was born in Perth, Western Australia. He was still a teenager when he moved to Sydney to try to make it as an actor. His tragic death in January 2008 made newspaper headlines and saddened many fans. He had finished filming his part as the Joker in the Batman movie, The Dark Knight, which was not yet released at the time of his death.

Phar Lap won many races, including the 1930 Melbourne Cup. Then he was shipped across the Pacific Ocean to race in Mexico. He won that race, too. Then something horrible happened. Phar Lap was suddenly very sick and died quickly. Some think he was poisoned. His death is still a mystery.

fun FACTS

Phar Lap was so important, his body was returned to Australia and mounted. It is on display in the Melbourne Museum.

Other Celebrities

Many people from Australia have become worldwide celebrities. Actress Nicole Kidman grew up near Sydney and still spends time with her family Down Under. America mourned the death of "Crocodile Hunter" Steve Irwin, who was killed by a stingray in 2006. His daughter, Bindi Sue Irwin, continues to appear on television to pass on his message of wildlife **conservation** (kon-ser-VAY-shun). Some other Australian celebrities are The Wiggles, country music star Keith Urban, and television actor Anthony LaPaglia.

Kangaroos are wild animals. People must get permission to keep them as pets. Some parks have tame kangaroos that children can feed by hand.

Abby Arrives

Chapter 5

We learned a lot about Australia—and just in time. On Abby's first day, she toured the school while we got the classroom ready to welcome her. Emma and I hung up our timeline. It spread all the way across the back of the room. Carrie and Patrick put up a big Australian flag. Our class had made it together. It was a fun project.

The Australian flag has the British flag (called the Union flag, or Union Jack) in the top left corner. The big star under the Union flag is the Commonwealth star. It stands for the original state of Australia. The other stars show the Southern Cross constellation. I've never seen that constellation. You can only see it when you are south of the equator.

Luke and I made ANZAC biscuits for snack time. They're like oatmeal cookies with coconut, but ANZAC

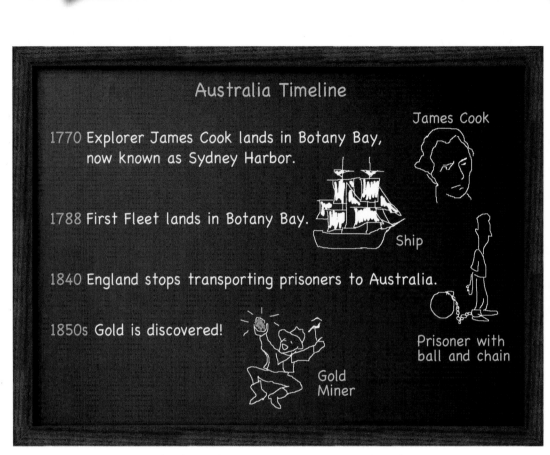

Beginning of Stacey and Emma's timeline

biscuits are more than just a yummy snack. They're called ANZAC biscuits because Australian and New Zealand soldiers ate them during World War I.

World War I began in 1914. ANZAC troops were fighting bravely overseas. Women back home were worried that the soldiers were not getting enough to eat. Food and other supplies were sent by ship, and it took a long time for them to arrive. Meat and vegetables would rot on the way.

The women needed a healthy food that would not spoil on the long sea voyage. That is how the recipe was invented. None of the ingredients (in-GREE-dee-unts) needed to be refrigerated to stay fresh.

Australian Flag

Church groups and schools made ANZAC biscuits to send to the soldiers. It was part of their country's war effort. People still bake and eat them Down Under.

I put our ANZAC biscuits on a tray just as Mrs. Young came in with our new student from Australia.

"G'day, mate!" we all shouted at once. I offered Abby the plate of cookies.

"My favorite bikkies," she said.

"Bikkies?" asked Luke.

"That's Australian for 'biscuits,' " explained Carrie. She had done her homework.

"And *biscuits* is Australian for cookies and crackers," I added. I had done my homework, too.

We asked Abby lots of questions. She told us about growing up in Townsville, Queensland, and spending lots of time at the beach. She was so lucky! Then she told us about the deadly Irukandji jellyfish at the

Abby stands next to a huge termite mound in northern Queensland. Mound-building termites are small insects, about the size of an ant. They live in Australia, Africa, and South America. Although the air outside is very hot, inside the mound, the air stays cool.

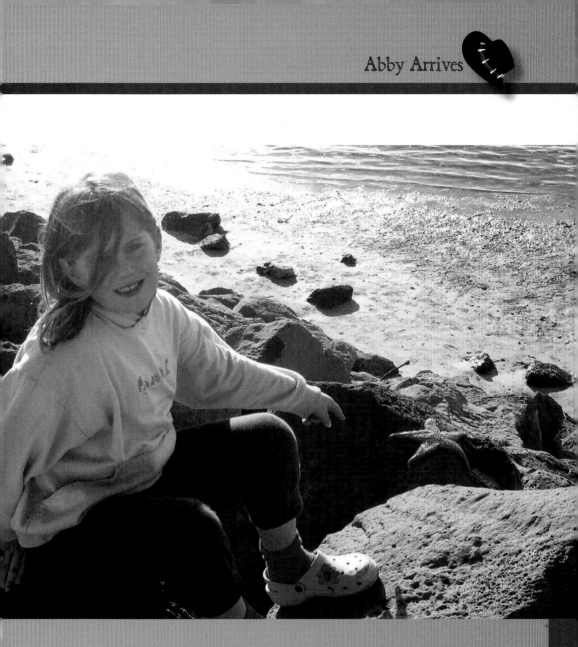

Abby spotted this big starfish when she was walking along St. Kilda Pier, near the city of Melbourne.

beach during summer. She wasn't stung, but she knew someone who was. He was rushed to the hospital and, luckily, lived.

Abby discovered this statue of a wombat at the Melbourne Zoo. Wombats are a close relative to koalas. They are active at night and sleep in underground burrows during the day.

"Okay, class." Mrs. Young got our attention. "Please take your seats."

I smiled as Abby took the seat next to mine. She smiled back, and I had a feeling she needed a new best friend, too.

How To Make

ANZAC
Biscuits

Instructions

1. Preheat the oven to 350°F.

2. Mix the flour, oats, coconut, and brown sugar in a large bowl.

3. Put the butter in a microwave-safe bowl and melt it on low in the microwave. Add the syrup or honey to the melted butter.

4. Put the baking soda in a small bowl. **Ask an adult** to add the boiling water. Stir, then add this mixture to the butter and syrup.

5. Pour these wet ingredients over the flour mixture and stir it all together.

6. Spoon the batter onto a cookie sheet. Leave room for them to spread out during baking.

7. Ask the adult to put them in the oven. Bake for about 15 minutes.

8. Let cookies cool. Store them in an airtight container.

Things You Will Need

Large bowl
2 small bowls
Spoon
An adult to help you
Cookie sheet
Oven

Ingredients

1 cup plain flour

1 cup rolled oats

1 cup shredded coconut (from package, not fresh)

1 cup brown sugar

½ cup (1 stick) butter

2 tablespoons golden syrup or honey

1 teaspoon baking soda

2 tablespoons boiling water

Make Your Own
Didgeridoo

You Will Need:

PVC pipe, 42 inches long, with
an inside diameter of 1.5 inches
(from a hardware store)

natural beeswax (from
a beekeeper, hardware
store, or health food store)

glass jar

sandpaper

The didgeridoo is believed to be the oldest wind instrument. To make didgeridoos, Aborigines would use tree branches that were hollowed out by termites. They would blow into the branch to make a droning sound, or they would tap the outside of the branch like a drum. The sound a didge will make changes with the length, shape, and thickness of the wood.

Instructions For Making
A Didgeridoo

1. Sand the ends of the PVC pipe until smooth.

2. Put a small piece of natural beeswax inside a glass jar and leave it in the sun for half an hour, or cook it in the microwave for 10 seconds.

3. When the beeswax is nice and soft, make it into a snake about a quarter inch thick. Press the beeswax snake in a circle onto one end of the pipe. Smooth and seal the inside of the mouthpiece. Then smooth and seal the outside. Work the beeswax until the hole is about 1 3/8 inch across. It can be slightly oval, but should be even, without any bumps.

4. Now you can play your didge. Press your lips against the beeswax and blow, letting your lips flutter loosely. Be sure to stay relaxed while playing to get the best sound.

Further Reading

Books

Arnold, Caroline. *Australian Animals*. New York: HarperCollins, 2000.

Davis, Kevin. *Look What Came From Australia*. New York: Franklin Watts, 2000.

Fowler, Allen. *Australia*. Millbrook, CT: Children's Press, 2001.

Heiman, Sarah, and Arturo Avila. *Australia ABCs*. Mankato, Minnesota: Picture Window Books, 2003.

Sayre, April Pulley. *G'Day Australia!* Brookfield, Connecticut: Millbrook Press, 2003.

Works Consulted

This book is based on the author's personal experiences in Australia and on the following sources.

ANZAC Biscuit Recipe
    http://www.aussieslang.com/features/anzac-biscuits.asp

The Australian Gold Rush
    http://www.cultureandrecreation.gov.au/articles/goldrush/

Australia History Timelines
    http://www.teachers.ash.org.au/jmresources/history/australian.html

Australian Indigenous Cultural Heritage: Australia's Cultural Portal
    http://www.cultureandrecreation.gov.au/articles/indigenous/

A History of Museum Victoria, 1932: Phar Lap
    http://www.museum.vic.gov.au/history/1932.html

"Kalgoorlie," *Sydney Morning Herald,* February 8, 2004
    http://www.smh.com.au/news/Western-Australia/Kalgoorlie/2005/02/17/1108500208500.html

Project Gutenberg of Australia
    http://gutenberg.net.au/timeline.html

Roberts, Greg. "Water Restrictions May Never End—Experts," *News Limited,* September 6, 2007,
    http://www.news.com.au/story/0,23599,22373479-29277,00.html

Further Reading

Syndey Olympic Games, 2000
http://www.cultureandrecreation.gov.au/articles/olympics/

On the Internet

Australia's Government
http://www.pm.gov.au/australia/government/history.cfm

EORC: Seen From Space, The Great Barrier Reef
http://www.eorc.jaxa.jp/en/imgdata/topics/2007/tp070425.html

Great Barrier Reef Facts: Plants and Animals
http://www.reef.crc.org.au/discover/plantsanimals/facts_plantanimal.htm

How to Play the Didgeridoo
http://www.didgeridoostore.com/howtoplay.html

The Phar Lap Story
http://www.pharlap.com.au/thestory

The Story of Gondwana
http://www.apstas.com/gondwanastory.htm

Uluru-Kata Tjuta (Ayers Rock—Mount Olga)
http://www.sacredland.org/world_sites_pages/Uluru.html

Embassy

Embassy of Australia, United States of America

1601 Massachusetts Ave, NW

Washington DC 20036

Telephone: (202) 797-3000

Fax: (202) 797-3168

http://www.austemb.org/

Glossary

Aborigines (aa-buh-RIH-jih-nees)—The first people of Australia.

ancestor (AN-ses-tor)—A relative who lived a long time ago.

colony (KAH-luh-nee)—An area governed by a distant country.

conservation (kon-ser-VAY-shun)—Managing natural resources in order to protect and save them.

continent (KON-tih-nent)—A large landmass (Earth has seven continents).

convict (KON-vikt)—A person who has been convicted of a crime.

democracy (deh-MAH-kruh-see)—A country with an elected government.

developed (dih-VEL-upd)—Having a high level of industry and employment.

didgeridoo (DID-juh-ree-doo)—A long, hollow wind instrument that has been used by Aborigines for thousands of years.

Down Under—A nickname for Australia because it is so far south, close to the "bottom" of the planet.

drought (DROWT)—A long time with little or no rain.

sacred (SAY-kred)—Holy; important to one's religion.

unemployment (un-em-PLOY-ment)—The number of people who can work but do not have jobs.

Index

ABOUT THE AUTHOR

Ann in a stinger suit, ready to go snorkeling at the Great Barrier Reef

Ann Weil is a freelance writer and world traveler. She lived "Down Under" for several years in New Zealand and Australia. Most of her time in Australia was spent in Queensland, near the Great Barrier Reef. Though very much a landlubber, she did venture out to the reef on several occasions to snorkel. Her memories of Australia include the kangaroos, of course, and the deafening dawn chorus of birds, louder than any alarm clock, which woke her up most mornings in far north Queensland.

Ann grew up in New York City and returned there after college to begin her career in publishing. She was a senior editor of series fiction for children, including the best-selling young adult *Sweet Valley High* series. She is the author of more than 50 books for children, including other titles in this series for Mitchell Lane Publishers.